Portraits of Bristol

by John Tompkins

Drawings by Grace D Bratton

Kingsmead

Kingsmead Press
Annesley House
21 Southside
Weston-super-Mare
Avon

ISBN 0 85026 001 9

AUTHOR'S NOTE
Prior reference to the Index Notes
before reading a particular poem may
be useful in understanding the historical background.

ACKNOWLEDGMENTS
The author wishes to acknowledge the great help
he has received from Helena Eason, the Bristol
historian, in the compilation of the historical
detail; and also to his wife for her unfailing
poetical criticism which invariably saves
the reader from most of the poet's worst licence.
Acknowledgments are also due to Patrick Wheare
of the Bath Evening Chronicle, and the B.B.C.,
who have printed or broadcast a few of the
items in the book.

Printed in Great Britain at The Pitman Press, Bath

Contents

Grace D Bratton
'77

The Merchant Venturers

'To Bristol! Aye! to Bristol
where the ships glide into town,
and all the luck a seaman needs
is 'Touch a Merchant's gown'.
To Bristol! Aye! to Bristol
with the sea wind in our hair,
to meet with Tom or Jenny
on the way to James's Fair[1] —
and maybe Moll of Christmas Steps
or Maddox[2] will be there . . .''

"A Canynges'[3] ship may sign us;
who knows what lies in store?
Cabot[4] has reached Newfoundland
and crews come by the score.
The hulks are leaving Bristol
for a world that grows as fast
as the dreams of every cabin boy
who sails before the mast . . .
And maybe we'll find riches
too vast to count our gains
— or maybe we'll get scurvy
and the rope's end for our pains!"

"But though the years may intervene
to keep us seas apart,
the tide that runs through Clifton Gorge
will ebb around our hearts . . .
and this I know, old shipmate,
I'll wager you and I
will take the road to Bristol
one day before we die . . .''

Neptune's Statue,
Bridgehead,
Broad Quay,
Bristol.

Clifton Suspension Bridge

Across the Gorge the man-made dream
is etched against the sky;
the cry of sea birds, far below,
is mingled with the slow,
insistent murmur of the rising tide.
A single ship slips by,
a silent toy returning home
that leaves a fringe of lace-edged foam
to lap the dark brown Avonside.

Brunel[1] — no less than Plimsoll[2] on the quay —
can rest content
to know how well their work was done.
The sun makes evening shadows
on the passing cars across the bridge
with tartan patterns
through the latticed steel;
you feel the trees across the way
will stay as sentinels
on guard throughout the night.

The autumn glory of the leaves
is burnished copper in the dying light,
until,
when time of celebration shall commend,
the moon pays homage
to the pendant lights that hang
a brilliant necklace, looping high,
across the Clifton sky . . .

Clifton Suspension Bridge,
The Portway,
Bristol.   7

Grace D. Bratton

Pay on the Nail!

Pay on the Nail![1]
Pay on the Nail!
— and never get into debt.
Neither cottage nor kingdom has ever surpassed
this old Bristol policy yet.
Pay on the Nail!
Pay on the Nail!
— or the deal is not really complete.
How can a man who is down on his knees
stand on his own two feet?

Brokers and whizz-kids or business tycoons
may amass unbelievable wealth,
but sadly I fear
it is perfectly clear
there's often a tax on their health.
They may make a million between 10 and 2,
on paper, at least, so they say . . .
But life's so uncertain
down 'Take-Over' way
they're broke by the end of the day!

Pay on the Nail!
Pay on the Nail!
As the old Bristolians would.
Show me the Chancellor,
modern 'enhance'-llor,
who ever did so much good . . .
Pay on the Nail!
Pay on the Nail!
Let those economists gape . . .
Get back to a ration
of 'Bristol Fashion'
— and Britain will be 'Ship Shape'![2]

**The Corn Exchange and
The Tower and Cupola of
All Saints Church.**

St Mary-le-Port Street, Old Bristol

When the aching twilight
of a summer's day
had passed away,
and the human tide
had ebbed and dwindled
to the faintest echo on a distant shore,
if you had gone
to stand alone
in silence in the quiet street,
you must have felt them brush
beside you as they passed
over the long-dead grass
on phantom feet.

Cavalier and fop
were there beside you in the shade
as the carriage rumbled on the cobbles to a stop;
and her skirts swished by you
as you stared
to share the homage
to the beauty of a day long-dimmed . . .
And surely you would feel the stir
of the buzz of talk that followed her?

The ancient, timbered houses,
whispered as they leaned
like aged spinsters, gossip wrapped,
above your head;
and you felt their tale had sped
across that narrow way
through countless ages,
and would clamber still
from gabled roof to crooked window sill
when *you* were dead.

And then there was a stirring in the breeze,
and the shouts of link-boys
seemed to beat about your ears;
and the years went rushing past you
'Til you'd hear a furious horseman
with the ringing of the hooves upon the stone . . .
and you were suddenly alone . . .
an atom in eternity.

St Mary-le-Port Street
used to run between
Bridge Street and
Wine Street near
The Old Dutch House.

Grace D. Bratton

The Council House, College Green

From unicorn to unicorn,
across the College Green,[1]
this arc of Civic Dignity
dominates the scene.
The Elizabethan seaman,[2]
beneath his central arch,
seems a little mystified
by 'Progress on the march' . . .
But will he not be reassured
to ponder on Ricart?[3]
By all those Royal Charters[4] —
or some historic part
of Bristol's 'Red Book'[5] saga,
six hundred years before
Chairman Mao[6] wrote down his 'thoughts' —
and turned them into law?

The cathedral watches over him,
with the chapel of St Mark.[7]
He knows the Lord Mayor's[8] 'arsenal'
protects him after dark —
with four majestic Swords of State,
silver maces (choice of eight!);
and even when 'protesters'
mass round him by the score,
he's able to defend himself
with the Water Bailiff's oar!

But though he may find life today
strange and more confused —
I wonder if 'Victoria'[9]
might even be 'amused' . . . ?

Grace D. Bratton '77

St Mary Redcliffe

Calm, majestic island
in a restless sea . . .
the 'fairest parish church in England'[1]
spurns the tide of traffic
lapping round her feet.
Where she would meet,
with gracious dignity,
A King or Queen or Merchant Prince,
she still retains
an ever-open door
for lonely wanderers
or needy poor.

Within these walls the soul of Bristol
prayed for guidance through the years;
the joys and tears
of ages past
have cast a silent benediction
over troubles of today.
Here rests the spirit of Divine content
that knits the timeless tapestry
from age to age
to clothe the aching emptiness
of those bereft.

Beneath the vaulted marvels
of the mason's skill,
the peace of centuries
descends as balm upon the sore distress
of mortal ills.
The shades of Southey,[2]
Coleridge, Cabot and Penn[3]
are all around.
Canynge, Colston, Wills and Fry[4]
stand waiting by to share
the certain solace to be found
where ageless miracles abound,
and even Bristol's tragic boy[5]
Found happy hours with 'Rowley'[6] to enjoy.

St Mary Redcliffe Church,
Redcliffe Way,
Bedminster.

Grace D. Bratton
'77

Clifton College Close[1]

The Cricket Match

The pitch is a ribbon of velvet,
    fresh in the morning air,
washed in the early sunlight —
    a hint of the dew still there.
The match is a great adventure
    as the umpire takes his stand,
the feel of the crimson leather
    is a dream in the bowler's hand.

He fingers the smooth enchantment,
    the seam is a wild delight;
    the ball is a mystic symbol
    carved for an ancient rite.
He measures his run to the wicket
    as a boy will step on the sand,
the mould of the shining leather
    is clay in the potter's hand . . .

For today is the day he dreamed of,
    when the ball is a living thing,
    swift as the flight of a falcon
    trained on a master's ring . . .
The pitch is a virgin parchment
    for a poet's eager pen;
and he feels with a breathless wonder
he could even take 'ALL TEN'[2] . . .

Clifton College and Close,
College Road,
Clifton.

Grace D. Bratton
'77

John Wesley

When revolution reared its ugly head
across the seas,
and France was ruled by Madame Guillotine;
when mean, poor hovels
were the miners lot
for ceaseless toil beneath the Kingswood[1] hill;
when poverty was still
the devil's advocate for crime,
and Newgate slime
spilled down the gutters of the poor[2] . . .
When all morality was more
a plaything for the rich,
and mortal sin
scarce worth a pennyworth of gin . . .

Then one man, wise beyond his time,
took up the torch that Whitefield[3] laid aside,
and with a humble, dedicated, pride
re-lit the dwindling fires of faith
to turn the loathsome tide.

For more than fifty years
he spread the gospel
like a living flame
to all who came
in thousands to respond
to Truth Incarnate, far beyond
the jungle of their daily lives.
From pulpit, horseback, open field,[4]
by sermon, written word and song,
he fought to right a million wrongs.
With brother Charles[5] he led the way
for multitudes to see
The Light of Christ
shine through His Word
to all eternity . . .

The John Wesley Statue
The New Room,
Wesley Chapel,
Broadmead,
Bristol.

Grace D. Bratton
77

Christmas Steps

To Whom it may Concern . . .

Dear Avon,
> Do you know
> that in your 'Gateway to the West'
> there rests a priceless pearl?
> Here in the very heart of town
> where traffic tides run high
> this peaceful, hidden haven
> can let the world go by . . .

> Three hundred years have almost run
> since this quaint 'streete was steppered done'.[1]
> Whilst Burke[2] and Colston,[3] close at hand,
> may, in their wisdom, understand
> the changing pressures of today,
> do they not sometimes sigh
> for tall, rigged sailing ships
> that moved like graceful swans
> beside the quay?
> . . . And we, on Christmas Steps,
> may still reflect, with thankful praise,
> on all the charm of bygone days . . .

> Fair Avon, what a heritage is ours
> to keep in trust . . .
> Let not the dust of passing years
> obscure the gifts that Time bestowed;
> none but the foolish would deny
> the worth of things man *cannot* buy . . .

Christmas Steps,
Colston Street,
Bristol.

Grace D. Bratton
'77

Song of Youth

The day is a new adventure;
I will bare my head to the sun,
I will live with the breeze
in the tenuous trees
'til the light of the day is done . . .

I will live *one* day in my lifetime
with the sunlight in my eyes,
with never a whispered "Ought I to?"
or social compromise.
I will take life as I find it
in country or in town;
I'll leave the reins in the hands of Youth,
I'll kill the cant and live the truth
and tear the pseudo down!

For did God make his masterpiece
to walk in prim, white, lines?
To trip around the edge of things
with little danger signs?
And did He give us life that we
daren't look it in the face?
And will He count the sum of things
to please the human race . . . ?

The University Tower and
City Museum and Art Gallery,
Queens Road,
Bristol.

St John's Gate

Said Brennus to Belinus,
"What a change this is from Rome!
Getting back to Bretaigne
is just like coming home . . ."
Then Belinus said to Brennus
"Why not build a city wall?
— unless, of course, you might prefer
to have a look at Gaul?"

"No, Beli, that's a good idea,
we'll start a little town —
I'm tired of sacking cities,
it's *time* we settled down!"

Said Beli, "Bren, I think you're *right*,
I *like* this little hill . . .
there's a time for honest fighting
— and a time for sitting still!
We'll name our town as 'Bristut';
let's make a little gate . . .
And, later on,
(when *we* have gone)
we still may sit in state,
upon a throne
carved from the stone,
whilst others may relate
the many things we *might* have done
. . . if *history* could wait!"

St John's Gate,
St John the Baptist Church,
Bottom of Broad Street, Bristol,
showing the statues to Brennus and
Belinus the legendary founders of Bristol. 25

Grace D. Bratton
'77

The Thatcher

The dawn was a whispered promise,
I was up and out with the sun,
over the shining, morning grass,
to see the wild hares run.
The day was a sea-washed pebble
in the eager hands of Youth,
and the way seemed clear before me
to eternities of truth . . .

But days are little lifetimes,
where roads are seldom straight,
and answers seem less simple
when the hour is getting late . . .
And then I turned a corner
where a thatcher plied his trade,
to see the sure and skilful way
each careful straw was laid.
How suddenly the winding road
was not so very long!
The day became a perfect whole
with birds at evensong . . .

For are our days not single straws,
in the Master Thatcher's hands?
each planned for our protection
. . . and He will understand.

The Dairy,
Blaise Castle,
House Museum of Social History,
Henbury, Bristol.

Grace D. Bratton

Bristol Zoo, Clifton[1]

In Memory of Alfred

"How odd can you get?"
said the ape with regret
as he peered through the bars of his cage.

"What strange looking objects they are to be sure
— with their ice creams and oranges well to the fore;
what a bore it must be
to have so little hair
they never stop thinking
of what they must wear!
Are those stilts on their heels
they stand on so much?
Their feet look deformed,
do they need a small crutch?
And what are those glass things most of the race
seem to have hanging in front of their face?
And why all the painting some of them do —
red on their lips and eyelids so blue?
Oh! well," said the ape sadly shaking his head,
"Perhaps it's *unkind* to call them ill-bred;
it may be they do it to keep out the cold,
or simply because they have never been told!
. . . but what impudent bounders
these humans must be . . .
to claim they have really
descended from ME!"

Bristol Zoo,
College Road,
Clifton, Bristol.

Grace D. Bratton

The Paragon

I stood upon The Paragon
and watched the Avon flow
beneath Brunel's great masterpiece
silently below.
Spring whispered in the gardens,
the dusk came dropping slow,
and all around there seemed to be
ghosts from long ago . . .

Cabot was slipping out to sea,
to land no-one knew where,
but the dreams of all Bristolians
were following him there.
I saw his little ship return,
the years all drifted by;
the mind will never hesitate
with orders for the eye . . .
and the river was a highway
with the merchants' sails unfurled
laden with rich cargoes
for America's New World.

William Penn seemed right beside me,
good Asbury[1] was there;
and Paul Revere[2] rode through the night
with something to declare . . .
Lincoln[3] came from Gettysburg,
Churchill[4] gave his sign . . .
and all the troubled future
suddenly look fine . . .

Cabot Tower, Brandon Hill

Upon this green and peaceful hill
the ragged edges of the mind
may find a new dimension
to the scheme of things;
for here we climb the foothills of eternity
and, age to age,
on Bristol's fascinating stage we see
today against the map of history.

Did not St Brendan[1] build a chapel here?
Recluse and hermit come and go?
Until a raging Henry[2]
tore the chapel down
to justify his crown?
And was Sebastian Cabot,[3]
as he has claimed,
born by this very place,
to leave for Venice at the age of four,
and then, once more return
with all his famous family?
And did not Rupert[4] dominate the town
when Cromwell sought to bring a monarch down
— until, two years[5] of siege away,
the 'Lord Protector' had his way?

All this and more
have added pages
to the endless book.
And when we look towards the tower,
etched like a minaret against the sky,
who many minds must wonder why
four hundred years had wandered by
before this stately edifice
was built to show
how John Cabot[6]
was Bristol bound
from new found lands
across the sea . . . . .

Cabot Tower,
Brandon Hill,
near Park Street,
Bristol.

Grace E. Bratton

The Little Things

When life is a dwindling melody
and youth an echo dying,
how will we dream of yesterday,
how will the memory climb
to the heights of happiness shrouded deep
in the gathering mists of time . . . ?

Will it be childhood we treasure most?
Or the white-hot flame of youth?
Or Deirdre's gossamer loveliness?
Or the passionate kiss of Ruth . . . ?
Will we remember best the days
when triumphs great or small
blazoned the hours with sudden pride?
Or will we first recall
days in the haze of a summer sun
down where the breakers fall . . . ?

I think we may, but most of all
as we dream through the dusty years,
the lingering song of the 'little things'
will mingle with the tears . . .
The turn of the lane where long ago
we found where the violets grow . . .
Or the smallest butterfly, azure blue,
carved on a milk-white stone . . .
Or the pool of liquid loveliness
a twilight street lamp showed
where a passing car
left a sudden star
of oil on a rain-wet road . . .

John Foster's Almshouses,[1]
Colston Street,
Bristol.

Grace D. Bratton
CC-77

Victoria Rooms

The cultural society
of Clifton, by the Downs,
was feeling quite frustrated
or wearing worried frowns
— and even Clifton ladies,
most politely, would complain,
"My dear, I fear
we're *buried* here
— where *can* we wear our gowns?
Daytime's not the problem . . .
we can grace the social scene
driving down Whiteladies Road
to stroll on College Green . . .
But *evenings* — Oh! those evenings!
with ballads by the score,
and dear Miss Jenkins dreadful harp —
twanging things in flat or sharp —
we *can't* take any more!"

So they formed a few committees
— with elegance and grace —
and bullied influential friends
to build a 'special place';
a place where they might gather
in fineries and lace . . .
And so it was that Dickens[1] came,
(Seat, lectern — glass as well!)
and even Mrs So and So
fell beneath his spell . . .
And then it was 'Aesthetics',
as seen by Oscar Wilde,[2]
so Important and *so* Earnest
. . . or perhaps to be reviled.

But let us not be sceptical,
— whatever caused their gloom —
our charming Clifton grandmamas
gave us these splendid rooms.[3]
Without their wish for culture
(at least that's what they said!)
some new, enchanting, office block
might now be there instead!

Victoria Rooms,
Queens Road,
Bristol.

Georgian Bar

Steak: Sole Pier
Steak: Duck Bar
Sherry Bar

64 Ye LLANDOGER TROW

Grace D. Bratton

Ye Llandoger Trow

Heave ho!
Llandoger Trow[1]
is waiting to take us aboard.
Heave ho!
Llandoger Trow
is ready for Llandogo hoard . . .
We're loaded with butter, cheeses and coal.
Down from the 'valleys' with Bristowe our goal,
straight from the Wye to the Severn we go,
we're bound for Ye Llandoger Trow.

Heave ho!
Boyo, boyo,
show what 'Red Dragons' can do!
Heave ho!
Boyo, boyo,
we'll tear the old Severn in two!
It's muddy, it's moody . . .
with *this* lot aboard,
Cwm Rhondda, me boyos,
and trust in the Lord!
— The Severn's no Heaven
for those who get *bored*![2]
We're bound for Ye Llandoger Trow.

Heave ho!
Llandoger Trow,
Welsh Back[3] is waiting to see
Llandogo cargoes — whatever they be —
the merchants will pay us
— It's Bristowe for we!
So pull hard, me boyos,
— all 'Dragons aglow' . . .
we're bound for Ye Llandoger Trow!

Ye Llandoger Trow,
King Street,
Bristol.

Grace D. Bratton
ᴁᴛ 77

Quakers Friars

Penn Street — to Pennsylvania
may seem a world away,
but talk with any Quaker
and hear what he will say.
Tucked away in Broadmead,
where Penn Street lies today
is still 'a meeting place for friends'
— with Bristol on display![1]

This Friary,[2] Dominican,
dissolved by Henry (eight)
was bought for re-development
(No planning made *them* wait!)
by enterprising City Guilds
— at least so it was said —
to sharpen up their City knives
to cut their Bristol bread.

And then in 1669,
when George Fox[3] came to stay,
thirty 'friendly' years went by
before that happy day
when William married Hannah[4]
— and took her far away.

And so from Quakers Friars
Pennsylvania got its name,
and William Penn with Hannah
earned immortal fame —
though some have heard
that George the Third[5]
held them both to blame!

Quakers Friars,
Broadmead,
Bristol.

Grace D. Bratton
'77

Bristol High Cross at Stourhead

How fare the kings[1] by Stourhead lake?
Who can decide
what memories surround the weathered stone?
Have they no haunting sense of loss
enthroned within their ancient cross?

Do they yet dream of Bristol days
when proudly they surveyed the town
— decreed as County by a grateful king?[2]
Do they still cling
to vestiges of Royal pride?
What can erase
the bitter banishment[3] of bygone days?
Do they still sigh for tall, proud ships
that sailed like summer clouds into the town,
whilst they looked down
upon the bustle of the scene
from College Green?
On winter nights
do they not speak of things
more clear to ancient kings
than mortal minds
can ever quite conceive?

Their Wiltshire garden is a wondrous thing,
each season brings
fresh glories to be seen . . .
Their sculptured majesties
now rest at peace,
secure, serene,
and all the crowded, medieval years
might not have been.

But may not Time's 'full circle'
change the theme of things?
Is Bristol not their natural home
— home fit for kings?

The Bristol High Cross,
Stourhead, Mere,
Wiltshire.
National Trust.

Index

the plague. The Nails were moved to their present position outside the Exchange designed in 1742 by John Wood, the Elder, when the pavement outside The Tolzey and the Council House — then across the road from The Tolzey — was altered in 1771. Payment by the merchants for bargains struck was made with money 'ON THE NAIL' — hence the expression.

2. 'SHIP SHAPE and BRISTOL FASHION' — the well-known phrase to denote a job well done.

The Council House — Page 13

1. The foundation stone was laid in 1935. When war broke out in 1939 the shell was almost finished. Finally opened by QUEEN ELIZABETH II in 1956.

2. THE ELIZABETHAN SEAMAN'S statue which stands under the central arch was designed by CHARLES WHEELER to represent JOHN CABOT but was not intended as a likeness.

3. The famous RICART'S MAIORES KALENDAR begun in 1479 by ROBERT RICART, Town Clerk, and continued as a perpetual history of each Mayor's year of office.

4. The archives of the city are housed here and include nearly 70 Royal Charters.

5. There is also THE LITTLE RED BOOK and THE GREAT RED BOOK containing the history of Bristol from 1344 until the end of the 16th century.

6. The late MAO TSE-TUNG the revolutionary leader of RED CHINA whose 'LITTLE RED BOOK', 'THE THOUGHTS OF CHAIRMAN MAO' became the revolutionaries 'bible'.

7. THE CHAPEL OF THE HOSPITAL OF ST MARK, across the road in Park Street, was founded in 1220. It was bought by the Corporation in 1541 and became the official place of worship for the Mayor and Corporation in 1721. It is now THE LORD MAYOR'S CHAPEL and is the only one in the country.

8. The Civic Insignia is kept in THE LORD MAYOR'S PARLOUR and includes 4 State swords, 8 silver maces, 2 silver trumpets, the Water Bailiff's silver oar and the 4 silver chains of the City Waits which bear the Tudor Badge of Queen Mary.

9. The statue of QUEEN VICTORIA stands at the apex of the triangular COLLEGE GREEN.

St Mary Redcliffe — Page 15

1. Described as "The fairest, goodliest and most famous parish church in England" by QUEEN ELIZABETH I in 1574.

2 & 3. The poets ROBERT SOUTHEY and SAMUEL COLERIDGE were both married in the church in 1795 to the sisters EDITH and SARAH FRICKER. SOUTHEY and EDITH — with her wedding ring hung round her neck, parted at the door. He sailed to Lisbon with his uncle whilst she went to stay with the sister of JOSEPH COTTLE the BRISTOL bookseller who earned enduring remembrance in literary circles by his financial help and encouragement to many later famous poets and writers. He actually paid for the ring worn by Edith. In spite of their most curious honeymoon their marriage proved much happier than that of the Coleridges who later separated for ever.

The memorial to ADMIRAL SIR WILLIAM PENN Kt. is most striking. He was appointed General and Commander of the Fleet in 1654 and was the famous father of the WILLIAM PENN who founded PENNSYLVANIA one of the original 13 states in the American Union 1681.

4. WILLIAM CANYNGE, merchant prince, who did so much to help the church. EDWARD COLSTON was probably the greatest benefactor Bristol ever had. He must have given hundreds of thousands of pounds to charitable purposes. There is a memorial window to him in the church. His arms of 2 dolphins biting an anchor are in the bottom left hand corner. LORD DULVERTON another great benefactor and a member of the WILLS FAMILY who did so much for the city undertook to defray the whole cost of exterior restoration and gave £85,000 in 1930 to make the church safe for generations to come. ELIZABETH FRY, was great as a SOCIAL REFORMER.

5. THOMAS CHATTERTON the poet son of a schoolmaster was born in the School House, Pile Street, opposite the church on 20th November 1752. Bristol's 'marvellous boy' of whom it has been said "He was the greatest genius England has produced since Shakespeare" died by self administered arsenic, starving in a London garret 24th August 1770. His short life was a classic example of unappreciated genius. The work he produced for quality and quantity was almost unbelievable by a boy of 17 years. Ironically, after his death, the now famous account book found in his pocket showed that although he had been literally starving for days he was owed £10.17.6 for contributions, a small part of which may well have prevented the final tragedy. The school house opposite the church is now kept as a memorial.

6. Many of CHATTERTON'S happiest hours were doubtless spent browsing through old documents in the Muniment Room of ST MARY REDCLIFFE and it was probably here that he first conceived the idea of the famous ROWLEY poems which he produced as the work of a 15th century monk. This he did so successfully that for years after his death the controversy as to the identity of their author still raged.

Clifton College Close — Page 17

1. CLIFTON COLLEGE, founded in 1862. Its many famous scholars include FIELD MARSHAL EARL HAIG, SIR MICHAEL REDGRAVE, TREVOR HOWARD, SIR ARTHUR QUILLER-COUCH and SIR HENRY NEWBOLT. During the 2nd World War the college was used as GENERAL OMAR BRADLEY'S H.Q. and now flies the STARS AND STRIPES on Independence day.

2. To take all ten wickets in an innings is every bowler's cricketing dream and very seldom realised. Something never achieved before — or since — took place on THE CLOSE and appears in THE GUINNESS BOOK OF RECORDS. It was here in 1899 that 'young Collins' scored the highest number of runs ever recorded in a single innings. Stretching over 5 afternoons he reached 628 Not Out. The feat is also recorded in WISDEN and in the PAVILION on THE CLOSE.

John Wesley — Page 19

1. His first open air preaching in Bristol was at The Brickfield on 2nd April 1739.

2. The Bristol Prison which like other NEWGATES of the time were infamous for their shocking conditions which prevailed.

3. GEORGE WHITEFIELD, the great revivalist predecessor of JOHN WESLEY who persuaded JOHN to continue his work with the rough colliers of KINGSWOOD before he left for America. He often preached to 20,000 but, like WESLEY was miserably persecuted. WHITEFIELD laid the foundation stone to the tabernacle in Penn Street in 1753.

4. JOHN WESLEY was the most remarkable religious force of the 18th Century. His open air methods were frowned upon by the Established Church, but his influence was undeniable. His Journals tell of his fantastic journey, mostly on horseback, often in appalling weather and road conditions. The NEW ROOM was established in the Horsefair in 1739, the first Methodist Chapel in the world. His journeys on horseback took him regularly to Bristol, Oxford, Newcastle, London, and all over the country. On his last visit to Bristol, when he was 87, he writes that he preached 'with no assistant, so I was obliged to shorten the service within the compass of 3 hours . . . .' He died in London in his 88th year. Bristol was among his last words. To his friends praying for him he said 'There is no need of more; when at Bristol my words were — I the chief of sinners am, but Jesus died for me . . .'

5. CHARLES WESLEY, brother of JOHN, is thought to be the greatest hymn writer who ever lived. Dr JAMES MARTINEAU, one of the most eminent ethical and philosophical writers of the 19th century has said: — 'after the scriptures, the WESLEY HYMNBOOK appears to me to be the grandest instrument of popular religious culture that Christendom ever produced.' CHARLES came to join JOHN in BRISTOL in 1749 and settled in CHARLES STREET, St James Barton for 20 years. Many of his children were born there and JOHN frequently lodged there when in Bristol. CHARLES WESLEY'S statue stands in the opposite courtyard of the Wesley Chapel to that of brother JOHN.

Christmas Steps — Page 21

1. At the top of the steps by Colston Street is a tablet that records: — 'This Streete was Steppered Done and finished Sept. 1669'. JONATHAN BLACKWELL, a wealthy London vintner who paid for it wished it to be called 'Queen Street' but it is now referred as to CHRISTMAS STEPS. In the 14th century it was named Cutler Street and Knife Street denoting the trades carried on and it was the old direct route from KINGS-DOWN to the CENTRE. At the foot of the steps is the ancient gateway to St Bartholomew's Hospital for old mariners. BRISTOL GRAMMAR SCHOOL was founded here 1532. At the top of the steps is the CHAPEL OF THE THREE KINGS OF COLOGNE and FOSTER'S ALMSHOUSES (See note with 'The Little Things . . .' poem).

2. EDMUND BURKE, politician, represented Bristol 1774—1780. A great intellectual statesman whose view of his political responsibilities went far beyond the wishes of some of his constituents. He felt that his time should be spent more at Westminster than canvassing at Bristol, and his championship of the American colonies, where he agreed entirely with Lord Chatham, displeased many Bristol merchants and led to the rupture with Bristol. He is acknowledged as one of the great legislators and his high principles have never been questioned. His statue stands on the Centre at Bristol.

3. EDWARD COLSTON the great Bristol philanthropist who has been described as 'the man of Bristol', was born 2nd November 1636 in Temple Street, the son of an eminent merchant. He followed his father's footsteps, trading chiefly in the West Indies. His crest of dolphins is said to be due to one of his ships springing a leak, a dolphin wedged itself in the hole and saved the ship. He lived chiefly in London but represented Bristol as M.P. for a short time and his many benefactions in the city show clearly where his interest lay. He never married and is reported as saying 'Every widow is my wife and every orphan is my child.' His gifts to Bristol were magnificent and included the Almshouses on St Michael's Hill, his help to

found and endow The Merchants Almshouses in King Street and his foundation of COLSTON SCHOOL which cost him £40,000. It was opened in 1710. He died in 1721 and his body was brought to Bristol from London in a hearse drawn by 6 horses, the 3 mourning coaches that followed were also drawn by 6 horses each. The procession took nearly 10 days, and he was interred in ALL SAINTS CHURCH, the bells of the city tolling for 16 hours. His effigy, by Rysbrach is in ALL SAINTS and a nosegay of flowers placed on the memorial every Sunday has been a charming tribute over the years to one of Bristol's most appreciative sons. His statue stands on the Centre not far from CHRISTMAS STEPS.

St John's Gate — Page 25

1. The 2 effigies of BRENNUS and BELINUS are carved above the gate. They were the legendary founders of Bristol who according to ROBERT RICART'S 'KALENDAR' 1479 (See note on COUNCIL HOUSE) led an army of Bretons and Gauls, sacked Rome B.C. 391 and then 'returned home into this lande of GRETE BRETAIGNE, with their Brettonnes, and dwelled here together in grete joye'.' Then BRYNNE first founded and billed this worshypful towne of BRISTUT, that is now BRISTOWE and set it upon a littel hill.'

   ST JOHN'S CONDUIT, now in NELSON STREET, was originally in BROAD STREET. It is a spring from BRANDON HILL which passes under PARK STREET. For a time during the blitz in 1940 it was the City's only water supply and has never dried up — even in the drought of 1976.

Bristol Zoo — Page 29

1. The Zoo covers 12 acres just beside BRISTOL'S famous DOWNS. It was opened to the public 11th July 1836, and has existed longer than any other Zoo in the U.K. and is the 5th oldest in the world. ALFRED the gorilla so beloved of visitors was 'in residence' 1930—48 until his death. His likeness has been preserved by the taxidermist in the BRISTOL MUSEUM and ART GALLERY. The Zoo is now rightly famous for its beautiful gardens and the only family of WHITE TIGERS in any Zoo in Europe.

The Paragon — Page 31

1. FRANCIS ASBURY. 'The Wesley of America' set out in 1771 to establish the first Methodist Chapel in New York.
2. PAUL REVERE the hero of the American Revolution who rode to Concord, Massachusetts with the fateful news of the uprising leading to independence in 1776.
3. ABRAHAM LINCOLN the great PRESIDENT OF U.S.A. who gave his famous 'Government of the people, by the people, for the people.' address at GETTYSBURG in the American Civil War.
4. WINSTON SPENCER CHURCHILL the legendary 2nd World War Leader and BRITISH PRIME MINISTER whose sign of two raised fingers showing 'V' for victory became a symbol of freedom throughout the over-run countries of Europe.

Cabot Tower, Brandon Hill — Page 33

1. Tradition says that ST BRENDAN (484—577) had a chapel here.
2. Recluses and hermits took possession of the chapel until HENRY VIII destroyed it during his purge of the monasteries.
3. SEBASTIAN CABOT, son of JOHN, claimed that he was born here but it has never been fully established.
4. PRINCE RUPERT took and held the city for the Royalists and occupied the camp on BRANDON HILL in the Civil War Sieges 1643—1645. Bristol, then reckoned to be the second city in the kingdom, was in the hands of The Parliamentary forces under Colonel NATHANIEL FIENNES, when Colonel HENRY WASHINGTON — ancestor of GEORGE WASHINGTON 1st PRESIDENT of U.S.A. saw a weakness in the defences between BRANDON HILL and WINDMILL FORT. With 300 dragoons he broke through and the Royalists took over the city. The spot where the breach was made is marked by a plaque outside the CITY MUSEUM.
5. Two years later, after months of siege, the Roundheads under GENERAL FAIRFAX took PRINCE RUPERT by surprise with a 2 a.m. attack and after fierce fighting the city fell to FAIRFAX.
6. THE CABOT TOWER was built 1897, exactly 400 years after JOHN CABOT sailed across the Atlantic to discover Newfoundland. It cost £3,300 and there are 109 steps to the top. On BRANDON HILL a quaint old tradition still exists that Bristol women can dry their clothes and beat their carpets there. A notice to that effect is posted on the Hotwells side of the hill.

The Little Things — Page 35

1. JOHN FOSTER, salt merchant, who lived in Small Street founded the CHAPEL OF THE THREE KINGS OF COLOGNE in 1504. It is a unique foundation and is only 18 feet by 22 feet. He left an endowment for the Almshouses which were founded for 13 men and women who were to receive 2d weekly. The almshouses were built over a period and rebuilt in the Burgundian style in 19th century. The Chapel is the original

architecture. JOHN FOSTER was SHERIFF OF BRISTOL 1474, MAYOR 1481 and M.P. 1489 and his statue rests in the charming courtyard at the top of CHRISTMAS STEPS.

Victoria Rooms — Page 37

1. In 1851 CHARLES DICKENS brought a fine company of actors to play at the rooms. He planned to produce two plays on the evening of 12th November. They were 'Not so bad as we seem' and 'Mr Nightingale's Dairy'. The cast also included WILKIE COLLINS and they played to a packed house. In response to appeals they gave another performance 2 days later.
2. OSCAR WILDE the great wit and playwright, possibly best known for 'THE IMPORTANCE OF BEING EARNEST.'
3. THE VICTORIA ROOMS were built in 1838.

Ye Llandoger Trow — Page 39

1. Was originally 5 merchants houses. The roof had 5 gables. It was built in 1664 and is one of the finest examples of 17th century timber framed houses in the city. It took its name from the flat bottomed barges known as TROWS (sometimes pronounced as in bough) which came regularly from LLANDOGO in Gwent, Wales — 8 miles from CHEPSTOW. These brought cargoes via the WYE RIVER, across the SEVERN, along the AVON into PILL harbour and then to WELSH BACK where the river is only a few yards from YE LLANDOGER TROW. The Inn was a favourite haunt of privateers, seamen of all kinds and customs officers. Its great cellars have doubtless held much contraband in bygone days. Some say it is the original of the Inn in 'TREASURE ISLAND'.
2. THE SEVERN 'BORE' is the wall of water that rushes along the river, most notably at the Spring and Autumn high tides. It can reach a height of 5 feet with a velocity of 14 miles per hour. The river SEVERN has a rise and fall of tide greater than any other river in Europe.
3. WELSH BACK HARBOUR, no doubt so named because of the regular cargoes arriving from WALES — to the cellars of YE LLANDOGER TROW.

Quakers Friars — Page 41

1. The old 'BAKERS HALL' now houses a permanent planning exhibition for Bristol with models, sketches, plans and diagrams for new development. It is open 1 p.m.—4.30 p.m. on WEEKDAYS.
2. Founded c. 1230.
3. GEORGE FOX, Founder of The SOCIETY OF FRIENDS, first came to Bristol in 1656 and married the remarkable MARGARET FELL — widow of JUDGE FELL — on 18th October 1669 in BROADMEAD CHAPEL. The Society included such famous names as THOMAS YOUNG — discoverer of undulatory theory of light — ELIZABETH FRY, JOSEPH LANCASTER, JOSEPH STURGE and from politics WILLIAM PENN, JOHN BRIGHT and GEORGE FOX.
4. HANNAH CALLOWHILL, a Bristol girl, was married here on 5th January 1696 to WILLIAM PENN the great coloniser and founder of PENNSYLVANIA U.S.A. They stayed in Bristol for 3 years before returning to America. The present hall was built 1747 by GEORGE TULLY and THOMAS PATY who had also designed WESLEY'S NEW ROOM.
5. GEORGE III was on the throne at the time of the American Revolution 1776. It is obviously quite untrue that he blamed WILLIAM PENN or HANNAH for his troubles. They were the great peacemakers.

Bristol High Cross at Stourhead — Page 43

1. THE BRISTOL HIGH CROSS was built to commemorate the granting of County Status to the city in 1373. It was placed at the crossroads of the 4 main streets. These were CORN STREET, HIGH STREET, WINE STREET and BROAD STREET. Originally the niches housed the kings who had been benefactors of the city — JOHN, HENRY II and EDWARD II. Afterwards EDWARD IV was added and in 1633 HENRY VI, ELIZABETH I, JAMES I and CHARLES I.
2. EDWARD III granted the charter 1373.
3. The career of THE BRISTOL HIGH CROSS to date has been almost stranger than fiction. In 1697 this fine example of 14th century craftsmanship was so well restored, coloured and gilded that it was said there was no better cross in the kingdom. Later a local silversmith feared that it might topple over in a high wind and damage his house. Astonishingly it was dismantled and left in the Guildhall Yard in pieces. Eventually it was rescued and erected again on COLLEGE GREEN. In 1763 it was dismantled once more and the reason given was that it 'interrupted gentlemen and ladies from walking ten abreast.' For some years it was left in a corner of the Cathedral grounds until DEAN BARTON gave it as a gift to his friend SQUIRE HOARE of STOUR-HEAD, WILTSHIRE! Six horse drawn wagons removed it to STOURHEAD and it has remained there ever since, in spite of various campaigns by Bristolians to try and arrange for its return. A reproduction was erected on COLLEGE GREEN in 1850 but was removed for QUEEN VICTORIA'S statue in 1888. A copy of the top section only is now to be seen in Berkeley Square.